Raising with Love

An Encouragement Guide for Parents and Caregivers

Vanessa Dargan

SJ Writing Services LLC
Publishing
Columbia, South Carolina
sjwritingservices.com

Copyright © 2025 by Vanessa Dargan
First Edition: 2025

Book Cover Design and Photography
J-Shots Photography & Media/Clinton.jones127@gmail.com

Editing
SJ Writing Services, LLC.

Testimonials

"*I loved everything about this book! It opened my eyes to things I never thought to include in my daily life as a mother. Raising with Love is such a valuable guide for parents, step-parents, and guardians trying to navigate parenthood. When I became a mom at 20, I had no idea what I was doing, but this book helped me understand so much about building strong bonds and raising my four kids with confidence. It's insightful, reassuring, and a must-read for every parent. 10/10!*"

Ronnell Straughn, Mother of 4

"*As a mother of four grown children and grandmother of three, I found this book to be both wise and empowering. Vanessa's thoughtful approach and practical strategies make this an invaluable guide for parents, grandparents, and caregivers alike. Her deep understanding of children's needs transcends experience, proving that empathy and expertise go hand in hand.*"

Allison Rashley, Mother of 4
Grandmother of 3, and Educator for 25+ years

Table of Contents

Dedication

To my parents—

Though life was not without its imperfections, I always felt the warmth of your love. Thank you for loving me the best way you knew how, for trying through the hard times, and for shaping me with your strength, your lessons, and your heart. I am who I am today because of both of you.

To my husband—

My steadfast encourager, my greatest supporter, and the love that steadies my dreams. You called me a teacher when I began this journey, and an author when this vision first took shape. Your unwavering belief reminds me that, always, love truly does win.

Chapter 1

Foundations of Love and Security

Every child's journey begins with love, trust, and safety. In this section, you'll explore the building blocks of strong relationships from showing love in ways children understand to teaching respect, forgiveness, and trust. These foundations help children feel secure and valued, regardless of the challenges they face.

<u>Love</u>

Love is the foundation of every healthy relationship. For children, feeling loved unconditionally shapes their confidence, resilience, and ability to love others.

Teaching Love Daily

- Express love with both words and actions.
- Show physical affection through hugs, cuddles, or handholding.
- Spend quality time together, phones and distractions put away.
- Practice patience, even in challenging moments.

Why Love Matters

- Builds trust and security.
- Teaches empathy, compassion, and kindness.
- Helps children manage stress and disappointment.
- Creates lasting family bonds that carry into adulthood.

Parenting Tips:

- Say *"I love you"* often, even when correcting behavior.
- Show love through small gestures: a note in their lunchbox, a favorite snack, or a smile.
- Remind them that love doesn't depend on achievements; it is constant.
- Let your actions mirror your words; children notice both.

Reflection Questions

- How do I show unconditional love to my child daily?

- What small gestures can I use to remind them they are cherished?

Love Languages

Every child gives and receives love in their own unique way. Understanding your child's "love language" helps you connect with them on a deeper level, making them feel truly seen and understood. A love language is both **how we like to be loved** and **how we naturally show love to others.**

There are five love languages: **Physical Touch, Quality Time, Acts of Service, Words of Affirmation, and Gifts.**

Physical Touch

- Hugs, cuddles, and holding hands.
- Gentle back rubs or shoulder squeezes.
- Sweet forehead kisses before bedtime.

Quality Time

- Uninterrupted time together, phones and distractions put away.
- Doing your child's favorite activity side by side.
- Asking them directly: *"What do you want to do together today?"*
- Special "son" or "daughter" dates one-on-one time that's just for them.

Acts of Service

- Asking, *"What would help you feel loved today?"*
- Redecorating their room together.

11

- Packing their lunches with care.
- Cooking their favorite homemade meal.
- Helping with projects or big chores.

Gifts

- Picking up their favorite snack as a small surprise.
- Allowing them to occasionally choose a special item from the store.
- Giving meaningful gifts, like a homemade card or something made just for them.

Words of Affirmation

- Saying, *"I'm proud of you," "You're such a kind person,"* or *"I believe in you."*
- Encouraging them with positive affirmations.
- Offering compliments about their efforts, talents, or appearance in ways that build confidence.

Parenting Tips:

- Have family conversations about how each of you likes to give and receive love.
- Never withhold a child's love language, even on tough days, they need consistency.
- If your child's language is "gifts," gently explain that gifts are occasional, not constant. Honesty helps them understand limits without making them feel less loved.

Reflection Questions

- Which love language does my child respond to most?

- How can I be intentional about showing love in the way they understand best?

Honesty

Honesty builds trust and integrity. When children learn to value truth, they grow into dependable, respectful, and trustworthy people.

Teaching Honesty

- Model honesty yourself, even in small things.
- Praise truth-telling, especially when it's difficult: *"Thank you for being honest, even though it was hard."*
- Create a safe environment so children don't feel they must hide the truth.
- Explain consequences clearly so they understand the importance of honesty.

Why Honesty Matters

- Builds stronger relationships at home and school.
- Creates a foundation of trust in friendships.
- Teaches accountability and responsibility.
- Protects children from the stress of keeping secrets or lies.

Parenting Tips:

- Avoid harsh punishment for mistakes, focus on the lesson learned.
- Talk about honesty in stories, books, or movies.
- Acknowledge your own mistakes honestly to model humility.
- Remind them: *"Even when you make mistakes, honesty keeps our trust strong."*

Reflection Questions

- How do I model honesty, even in small things?

- How can I create safety so my child feels they can always tell the truth?

Apologizing

Apologies are powerful—they teach children the importance of accountability, healing, and caring for relationships. Just like love languages, everyone has a way they feel most understood through an apology.

The five apology languages are: **Expressing Regret, Accepting Responsibility, Restoring, Planning Change, and Asking for Forgiveness.**

Expressing Regret

- Saying, *"I'm sorry."*
- Naming the emotion: *"I'm sorry I made you feel angry,"* or *"I'm sorry I hurt your feelings."*
- Show your child that you understand how your actions affected them.

Accepting Responsibility

- Admitting when you were wrong.
- Saying, *"I take full responsibility."*
- Avoid excuses or shifting blame.

Restoring the Relationship

- Asking, *"How can I make this right?"*
- Following up with genuine action, not just words.

Planning Change

- Commit to doing better next time.
- Example: If raising your voice upsets your child, promise to practice speaking calmly when you feel frustrated.

Asking for Forgiveness

- Saying, *"Can you forgive me?"*
- Allowing your child time to process healing takes patience.

Parenting Tips:

- Learn your child's "apology language," just like their love language.
- Always apologize when you are in the wrong. It models healthy humility.
- Show sincerity; children know when words are empty.

Reflection Questions

- How do I usually apologize to my child?

- What apology language seems to mean the most to them?

Respect

Respect means showing care for yourself, for others, and for the world around you. Children learn respect first by being respected at home.

Respect for Self
- Listening to your own feelings and trusting your instincts.
- Building confidence by valuing yourself.
- Protecting yourself from harmful words and actions.
- Saying your needs with clarity and kindness.

Respect for Others
- Honoring parents, teachers, and leaders who offer guidance.
- Appreciating differences in race, culture, values, and beliefs.
- Remembering the "Golden Rule": *Treat others the way you want to be treated.*

Parenting Tips:
- Model respect in everyday life, greet strangers politely, show gratitude, and listen with care.
- Use real-life examples, such as at the grocery store, with family, or when meeting new people.
- Show your child what respectful body language looks like, maintaining eye contact, smiling, and speaking in a calm voice.
- Praise respectful actions when you notice them in your child.

Reflection Questions

- How do I show respect to my child in everyday life?

- How can I teach them to respect both themselves and others?

Morals & Values

Morals are knowing right from wrong. Values are the personal beliefs that guide our lives. Teaching both helps children grow into kind, responsible, and thoughtful people.

Teaching Morals and Values

- **Model Good Behavior:** Children learn more from what you do than what you say. Show honesty, respect, and compassion.
- **Apologize When Wrong:** Saying *"I made a mistake, and I'm sorry"* teaches humility and respect.
- **Share Personal Stories:** Tell your child about times you made tough choices and what you learned.
- **Encourage Responsibility:** Hold children accountable for their actions in loving, age-appropriate ways.
- **Promote Perseverance:** Remind them that quitting isn't the answer; finishing challenging tasks builds strength and resilience.
- **Teach Kindness:** Encourage acts of service, like helping a classmate or befriending someone new.

Parenting Tips:

- Talk regularly about what's right and why.
- Praise moral choices: *"I'm proud you told the truth, even though it was hard."*
- Establish clear family rules, such as honesty, kindness, and respect.
- Allow mistakes to become learning opportunities.

25

Reflection Questions

- What values are most important in my family?

- How can I model honesty and kindness daily?

__Obedience__

Obedience is about listening, respecting guidance, and taking responsibility. It's not about fear; it's about trust and learning.

Teaching Obedience with Love

- Explain the *why* behind the rules so children understand, not just obey.
- Use calm and consistent expectations.
- Praise cooperation and respectful listening.
- Be patient—obedience grows with time and practice.

Why It Matters

- Helps children stay safe.
- Builds respect for authority figures, such as parents, teachers, and community leaders.
- Prepares them for teamwork and responsibility.
- Teaches self-discipline and accountability.

Parenting Tips:

- Avoid yelling or harsh punishments; gentle consistency is most effective.
- Show respect when correcting: kneel to eye level, use a calm tone, and explain the issue clearly and concisely.
- Celebrate small acts of obedience: *"Thank you for listening the first time I asked."*
- Model respect for rules in your own life; children learn by watching.

Reflection Questions

- How do I teach obedience through love and respect?

- What routines can help my child practice listening well?

<u>Forgiveness</u>

Forgiveness is an act of love—both for yourself and for others. It enables children to release hurt, find peace, and rebuild trust in their relationships.

Teaching Forgiveness

- Show empathy: *"I understand why you feel this way."*
- Let children know their feelings are valid, they're allowed to feel angry, sad, or hurt.
- Remind them that forgiveness doesn't mean forgetting; it means choosing peace over resentment.

What Forgiveness Brings

- Freedom and peace of mind.
- Healing of relationships.
- Greater understanding and compassion.

What Happens Without Forgiveness

- Lingering anger or resentment.
- Replaying conflicts in their minds.
- Broken trust or strained relationships.
- Restless emotions and stress.

Parenting Tips:

- Model forgiveness in your own life, say out loud, *"I forgive you."*
- Encourage children to express emotions in healthy ways (crying, talking, journaling).
- Show them that forgiveness takes courage and brings relief.

Reflection Questions

- What does forgiveness look like in my family?

- How can I model letting go of anger for my child?

Trust

Trust is the foundation of every healthy relationship. Children who learn to trust feel safer, more confident, and more connected to the people who love them.

Building Trust

- Keep promises, even small ones.
- Be honest with your children, even when the truth is complicated.
- Show consistency; your reliability makes them feel secure.
- Model integrity: do what you say you'll do.

Breaking and Repairing Trust

- Trust can break through lies, broken promises, or harsh actions.
- Rebuilding requires patience, time, and consistent effort.
- Talk openly about what happened and how to move forward.

Parenting with Trust

- Give children safe chances to prove their responsibility.
- Share your worries gently instead of over-controlling.
- Ask open-ended questions that demonstrate that you value their thoughts.
- Celebrate honesty, even when it's hard to tell the truth.

Parenting Tips:

- Be a model, apologize when you break trust in yourself.
- Keep private conversations confidential when your child asks.
- Allow age-appropriate independence to show them you believe in them.
- Remind them: *"Even when mistakes happen, my love for you doesn't change."*

Reflection Questions

- How can I build trust with my child through daily vacations?

- How do I repair trust when it's broken?

Chapter 2

<u>Emotional Well-Being</u>

As children grow, they experience a range of intense emotions and learning how to understand and manage them is essential. This section focuses on helping children develop empathy, patience, and gratitude, enabling them to build resilience and confidence. With your support, children learn that all feelings are welcome and that they are never alone in them.

Emotions

Helping children understand and express their emotions builds confidence, empathy, and resilience. Emotional intelligence is just as important as academic skills.

Teaching Emotional Awareness

- Expand their emotional vocabulary beyond "happy, sad, mad." Introduce words like "frustrated," "excited," or "disappointed."
- Ask questions to help them connect feelings to events: *"What made you feel that way?"*
- Encourage them to share their feelings without fear of being judged.
- Show them healthy ways to manage their emotions, such as drawing, journaling, deep breathing, or talking.

Supporting Healthy Expression

- Let children know all feelings are normal, but not all actions are okay.
- Show empathy: *"I understand you feel upset."*
- Provide a calm space for cooling down when emotions run high.

Parenting Tips:

- Model emotional honesty, share your own feelings, and how you cope with them.
- Validate emotions rather than dismiss them.

- Avoid shaming or mocking feelings; this teaches children that emotions are safe to express.
- Step away when emotions are too high and return when calm to continue the conversation.

Reflection Questions

- How do I respond when my child expresses big feelings?

- What tools can I give them for healthy emotional expression?

<u>Empathy</u>

Empathy is the ability to understand and share another person's feelings. It's the foundation of compassion, kindness, and healthy relationships.

Nurturing Empathy at Different Ages

Ages 3–5

- Label emotions: *"You look upset. Are you feeling sad?"*
- Notice body language: *"You stomped your feet—you seem angry."*
- Ask how others might feel in certain situations.

Ages 5–7

- Use pictures of faces to discuss emotions.
- Encourage playing with children from different backgrounds.
- Read diverse stories and ask, *"How do you think this character feels?"*

Ages 7–9

- Have deeper conversations about perspectives.
- Play team games or activities that require cooperation.
- Encourage respectful debates where participants consider different viewpoints.

Ages 9–12

- Discuss real-world events and ask, *"How would you feel if that happened to you?"*
- Encourage volunteering or service projects that connect them to others' needs.

Parenting Tips:

- Respect your child's boundaries while teaching them to respect others'.
- Remind them they don't have to solve everyone's problems, but they can always show care.
- Model empathy in daily life by listening closely, offering kindness, and honoring others' feelings.

Reflection Questions

- How can I help my child recognize the feelings of others?

- What daily practices can nurture empathy at home?

Patience

Patience is the ability to wait calmly, even when we desire something immediately. It teaches children self-control, resilience, and respect for others.

Teaching Patience
- Practice waiting with small things like taking turns in a game or standing in line at the store.
- Praise them when they wait without complaining.
- Use stories, examples, or role-play to show the value of patience.

Why Patience Matters
- Builds stronger relationships.
- Helps with problem-solving and decision-making.
- Reduces stress and frustration.
- Makes big goals feel achievable, one step at a time.

Parenting Tips:
- Model patience in your own life, let them see you take deep breaths when frustrated.
- Avoid instant gratification; sometimes waiting teaches valuable lessons.
- Use phrases like *"Good things take time"* or *"Let's wait together."*
- Celebrate moments of patience with hugs, high-fives, or kind words.

Reflection Questions

- How do I model patience in my daily life?

- What small opportunities can I give my child to practice waiting?

Decision-Making

Decision-making is a skill that grows with practice. When children learn to make thoughtful choices, they gain confidence and independence.

Teaching Good Decision-Making

- Start with small decisions: what to wear, what snack to eat, or which game to play.
- Discuss options and potential outcomes together.
- Teach the difference between quick decisions (such as what to wear) and important ones (like how to spend money).
- Encourage children to pause and think before acting.

Why It Matters

- Builds responsibility and problem-solving skills.
- Helps children handle peer pressure with confidence.
- Prepares them for bigger life choices as they grow.

Parenting Tips:

- Support their decisions, even if they choose differently than you.
- Share your own decision-making process out loud.
- Remind them that mistakes are learning opportunities, not failures.
- Encourage reflection: *"How did that choice work out for you?"*

Reflection Questions

- What small decisions can I let my child make today?

- How can I support them when their choices don't go as planned?

Gratitude

Gratitude is the practice of noticing and appreciating the good around us. Teaching it helps children grow into happier, more content, and compassionate people.

Ways to Teach Gratitude

- Model saying "thank you" often, both at home and in public.
- Keep a family gratitude journal—write down one thing you're thankful for each day.
- Pause at meals to share something you appreciate.
- Encourage children to write thank-you notes for gifts or kind gestures.

Benefits of Gratitude

- Increases happiness and resilience.
- Builds stronger relationships.
- Reduces entitlement and envy.
- Helps children focus on what they have, not what they lack.

Parenting Tips:

- Turn gratitude into a daily habit; bedtime or dinner are great times to reflect.
- Celebrate small moments: a sunny day, a hug, a favorite meal.
- Teach gratitude not only for things, but for people and experiences.
- Remind your child that gratitude often leads to kindness in action.

Reflection Questions

- What daily gratitude practice can we do as a family?

- How can I show my child that gratitude is more than saying thank you?

Self-Esteem

Self-esteem refers to the way children perceive and value themselves. When it's nurtured, they grow confident, resilient, and ready to face life's challenges.

Building Healthy Self-Esteem

- Praise effort, not just results: *"I'm proud of how hard you worked."*
- Encourage independence by letting them try new things.
- Teach them that mistakes are part of learning, not signs of failure.
- Celebrate their unique strengths, talents, and qualities.

Signs of Low Self-Esteem

- Negative self-talk (*"I'm not good enough"*).
- Avoiding new activities or challenges.
- Seeking constant approval.
- Struggling with friendships.

Parenting Tips:

- Model positive self-talk in your own life.
- Give children responsibilities that demonstrate your trust in them.
- Avoid harsh criticism, correct gently, and encourage growth.
- Remind them often: *"You are valuable just the way you are."*

Reflection Questions

- How do I build my child's confidence daily?

- What words of encouragement can I use more often?

Chapter 3

Healthy Relationships and Boundaries

Respectful, safe relationships give children the tools to thrive in community with others. In this section, you'll find guidance on communication, boundaries, consent, body autonomy, and more. These lessons empower children to build trust, practice kindness, and form healthy connections throughout their lives.

<u>Communication</u>

Good communication builds connection, confidence, and trust. Children who feel heard are more likely to share openly with parents, teachers, and trusted adults.

At Home

- Teach the importance of maintaining eye contact and using open body language.
- Involve your children in age-appropriate conversations. This shows their voice matters.
- Allow them to share feelings without judgment or dismissal.
- Provide safe adults they can confide in, such as grandparents, teachers, or babysitters.

At School

- Encourage children to speak up when they're struggling with classmates, teachers, or schoolwork.
- Remind them that many caring adults at school (teachers, counselors, nurses) are ready to listen.

Parent–Teacher Communication

- Build a positive partnership with teachers.
- Let children participate in conferences so they see it as a safe and supportive space.
- Share feedback, concerns, and encouragement openly.

Parenting Tips:

- Set aside weekly time for meaningful talks at dinner, during a walk, or before bed.
- Ask open-ended questions like, *"What was the best part of your day?"*
- Practice active listening by nodding, maintaining eye contact, and repeating back what you have heard.
- Remind them that honest communication makes them stronger and more connected.

Reflection Questions

- How often do I pause to truly listen to my child?

- What can I do to help them feel safe sharing openly?

Boundaries

Boundaries help children understand their comfort levels and how to protect themselves in relationships. Teaching boundaries early builds self-respect and healthier connections with others.

Types of Boundaries

- **Emotional:** Choosing how much personal information to share.
- **Time:** Managing time between play, chores, and responsibilities.
- **Intellectual:** Respecting different opinions while holding onto your own.
- **Material:** Deciding what belongings can or cannot be shared.
- **Physical/Sexual:** Understanding consent and respecting personal space.

Supporting Your Child's Boundaries

- Ask your child what boundaries matter most to them.
- Listen carefully and honor their needs.
- Explain that everyone's boundaries look different and that's okay.
- Model your own boundaries as a parent and gently explain consequences.

Parenting Tips:

- Role-play scenarios to practice assertiveness. Example: *"I don't like it when you take my things without asking. Please ask next time."*
- Teach them to say "no" with confidence.
- Show respect for their boundaries at home, it strengthens trust and fosters a healthy relationship.
- Let them see you say, "No." So, they learn it's a healthy thing to do.

Reflection Questions

- How can I respect my child's boundaries while teaching them to respect others?

- What healthy boundaries can I model in my own life?

Consent

Consent is about respect, it means asking for permission before acting and honoring the answer, whether it's yes or no. Teaching consent early helps children establish safe and healthy relationships.

Everyday Consent

- Model "permission seeking" in daily life: *"Can I borrow your pencil?"* or *"Would it be okay if I posted this picture of us?"*
- Show your child that consent isn't just about big things; it's a part of everyday kindness and respect.

Accepting "No"

- Teach children that it's okay for others to say no—and that it's okay for them to say no, too.
- Remind them that "no" doesn't mean rejection, it just means setting healthy boundaries.

Saying "No" Confidently

- Practice scenarios where they must say no and discuss possible outcomes.
- Model saying no firmly but kindly as a parent it teaches them strength and respect.
- Be consistent with your own boundaries so children learn that "no" is final and healthy.

Parenting Tips:

- Ask for your child's consent for small things, such as hugs or borrowing their belongings.
- Praise them when they respect someone else's boundaries.
- Use real-life moments as gentle teaching opportunities.

Reflection Questions

- How do I teach my child to ask permission and honor others' boundaries?

- What opportunities do I give them to practice saying no?

Body Autonomy

Body autonomy means every person has the right to make choices about their own body. Children who understand this grow up knowing their body belongs to them and that they have the power to set boundaries.

Teaching Body Autonomy

- Remind your child, *"You are the boss of your own body."*

- Never force hugs, kisses, or physical affection, not even with family. Offer alternatives like a wave, fist bump, or high-five.

- Teach them to ask before touching others, too: *"Can I give you a hug?"*

Safe Adults

- Help children identify trusted adults they can go to for help.

- Remind them that safe adults will always listen, respect their choices, and never make them feel uncomfortable.

Using Correct Terms

- Teach children the proper names for body parts. This gives them confidence to speak up if they ever need to.

Parenting Tips:

- Model respect for their personal space, knock before entering their room, and honor their comfort levels.

- Reinforce that their body is theirs, always.

Reflection Questions

- How can I reinforce that my child's body belongs to them?

- What examples can I model to show respect for autonomy?

Sexual Health

Sexual health is more than "the talk" — it's an ongoing conversation about respect, consent, safety, and self-worth. When caregivers speak openly and honestly, children learn to view their bodies and relationships with confidence and care.

Guiding with Respect and Care

- Start early with simple, age-appropriate lessons about body parts and personal safety.
- Normalize conversations about puberty, relationships, and consent as children grow.
- Emphasize that sexual health includes respect for self and others.
- Emphasize values such as kindness, responsibility, and safety in relationships.

Consequences of Poor Sexual Health

Physical Health Consequences

1. **Sexually Transmitted Infections (STIs)**

- Includes HIV, chlamydia, gonorrhea, syphilis, herpes, HPV
- Can lead to chronic illness, infertility, and organ damage

2. **Unintended Pregnancies**

- It can impact physical health, especially if prenatal care is lacking.

- May increase maternal mortality and complications

3. **Infertility**

- Often a result of untreated STIs (e.g., chlamydia, gonorrhea)

4. **Cancer Risks**

- HPV is a leading cause of cervical, anal, and throat cancers

For more detailed information about sexual health, please refer to the resources page

Parenting Tips:

- Answer questions honestly—if you don't know, learn together.
- Teach consent early: *"Your body belongs to you, and you deserve respect."*
- Create a safe and nonjudgmental space for conversations about identity, relationships, and personal choices.
- Remind them: *"You never need to be ashamed of your questions — I'll always listen with love."*

Reflection Questions

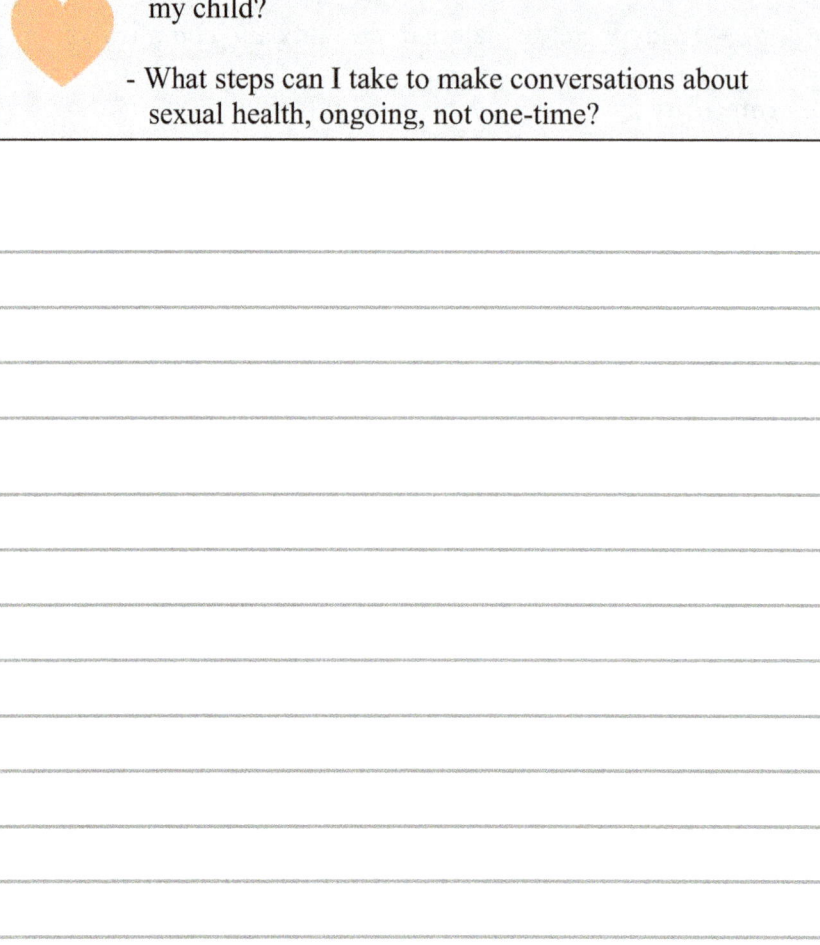

- How do I model healthy, respectful relationships for my child?

- What steps can I take to make conversations about sexual health, ongoing, not one-time?

Relationships

Healthy relationships are built on trust, respect, and kindness. Teaching children about relationships early helps them recognize what feels safe and supportive.

Teaching About Relationships

- Model respect and healthy communication in your own relationships.
- Discuss openly the importance of boundaries, trust, and honesty.
- Encourage friendships that are uplifting, supportive, and fun.
- Remind them that relationships should never feel controlling or hurtful.

Building Relationship Skills

- Teach conflict resolution—listening, compromising, and apologizing.
- Encourage empathy by asking: *"How do you think they feel?"*
- Help them recognize red flags, such as dishonesty, manipulation, or disrespect.

Parenting Tips:

- Keep conversations ongoing as children grow into teens and young adults.
- Create a safe space for them to ask questions about friendships or dating.
- Celebrate their healthy choices in relationships.
- Remind them: *"You deserve to be treated with respect and love."*

Reflection Questions

- How do I model respect and kindness in relationships?

- What safe conversations can I create about friendships and dating?

Marriage

Marriage, for those who choose it, is a partnership built on love, respect, and commitment. Teaching children about healthy marriages helps them form realistic expectations and lays a strong foundation for the future.

What Makes a Healthy Marriage
- Communication that is honest, respectful, and kind.
- Commitment through good times and hard times.
- Teamwork, sharing responsibilities, and supporting each other's dreams.
- Forgiveness and patience when mistakes happen.

Teaching About Marriage
- Share positive examples from your own life or others they admire.
- Be honest that marriage takes work, not just love.
- Encourage them to value themselves so that they choose partners who value them as well.
- Highlight that marriage is a choice, not a requirement for a happy life.

Parenting Tips:
- Model healthy conflict resolution and mutual respect in your relationships.
- Talk openly about love, commitment, and partnership.
- Remind them: *"A strong marriage is built on friendship, respect, and unconditional love."*

Reflection Questions

- What healthy marriage or partnership lessons can I

- How do I teach my child that love is built on respect
  and teamwork?

Chapter 4

<u>Resilience & Growth</u>

Life is filled with challenges, and children need strong roots to weather difficult seasons. This section offers encouragement and practical tools for navigating divorce, grief, trauma, and mental health. With compassion and steadiness, you can help your child heal, grow, and find hope even in the most challenging times.

<u>Divorce</u>

Divorce is never easy for parents or for children. It's a significant change that can evoke a range of emotions. However, with honesty, respect, and open communication, children can feel secure and loved, even as their family undergoes changes.

Talking With Your Children

- Share plans with your child as a parent whenever possible. When children hear the same message from both of you, they feel safe and included.
- Let your children know about changes early on, in ways they can understand. A simple, honest explanation helps prevent confusion.
- Invite them to share their feelings or preferences when appropriate. Even small choices, such as decorating their new room or selecting a holiday tradition, can help them feel valued.
- Be open about your own emotions. It's okay for your kids to see that divorce is sad or difficult for you, too. It shows them it's normal to have feelings.

Creating Stability

- Work together to create routines that feel steady and predictable for your children. Routines give them comfort and a sense of safety.
- Talk clearly about practical plans:

- Which parent is moving, and where?
- How holidays will be celebrated.
- Custody schedules and transitions between homes.

- For children over 18, respect their ability to make their own choices while still offering guidance and love.

Supporting Emotional Health

- Remind your children that all feelings, mad, sad, angry, confused, hurt, are okay, and none of this is their fault.
- Show them healthy coping tools, such as journaling, drawing, playing outside, or talking one-on-one.
- Check in often: "How are you feeling about things this week?" A regular rhythm of gentle conversations helps them feel cared for.
- Always choose honesty over hiding the truth. Lies or half-truths create more fear than clarity.

Building a Healthy Co-Parent Relationship

- Speak respectfully to one another in front of your children. They will mirror how you treat one another.
- Practice calm communication: gentle tones, kind words, and body language that shows respect.
- Continue to show your children that both parents love them deeply, even if your relationship with each other has changed.

Parenting Tips:

- Use a shared calendar so your children know what to expect.
- Tell your children about schedule changes in advance.
- Let them see that you and their other parent still value and respect each other.

Reflection Questions

- How can I reassure my child that both parents will always love them?

- What routines can I create to give my child a sense of stability?

Healing from Trauma

Trauma can make a child feel broken, unsafe, or even responsible for what happened, but it's never their fault. Healing is possible with love, patience, and support.

The 3 R's of Healing

- **Reassure:** Remind your child they are safe and deeply loved. Use gentle words, hugs, or extra one-on-one time to bring comfort.
- **Return to Routine:** Maintain your daily schedules as close to normal as possible. Consistency helps children feel secure and grounded.
- **Regulate:** Teach calming tools like deep breathing, stretching, drawing, or playing outside. These help them manage big feelings in healthy ways.

Tools for Healing

- Create safe spaces at home, such as a cozy chair, a small tent, or a quiet corner.
- Offer comforting items such as a nightlight, a soft blanket, or calming music.
- Encourage creative outlets like art, journaling, or dance.
- Stay connected through supportive relationships such as trusted adults, teachers, or friends.
- Consider professional therapies (art, play, or counseling) when needed.

Parenting Tips:

- Stay calm during your child's emotional storms. Kneel to their level, speak gently, and reassure them they're not alone.
- Model healthy coping strategies—let them see you take deep breaths, go for a walk, or talk through your feelings.
- Remind them often: *"You are safe, it's not your fault, and you are loved."*

Reflection Questions

- How can I reassure my child that they are safe?

- What calming tools can I teach them to regulate big emotions?

Grief

Grief is the natural response to losing someone or something we love. For children, it can feel confusing, heavy, and overwhelming. Your love and honesty will help them heal.

Signs of Grieving in Children
- Sadness, fatigue, or withdrawal from friends.
- Nightmares, loss of appetite, or frequent stomachaches.
- Asking repeated questions about the person who died.
- Reverting to earlier behaviors like thumb sucking or bed-wetting.

Supporting a Grieving Child
- Be honest but gentle: say *"died"* instead of "went to sleep."
- Let them ask questions and share their fears.
- Maintain routines as normal as possible to maintain a sense of stability.
- Allow them choices in how they remember their loved one.
- Be patient, grief often returns in waves as children grow.

Parenting Tips:
- Expect grief to resurface around birthdays, anniversaries, or other significant milestones, and holidays.
- Be present, your calm presence is more powerful than perfect words.
- Encourage healthy expression through activities such as drawing, storytelling, or play.

Reflection Questions

- How can I help my child remember a loved one with love and comfort?

- What healthy outlets can I encourage during times of grief?

Therapy

Therapy provides children with a safe space to express their feelings, learn coping skills, and heal from their struggles. It's not a sign of weakness it's a powerful tool for growth.

Who's Involved?

- **One-on-one therapy:** the child and therapist work together.
- **Parent-focused therapy involves parents meeting** with the therapist.
- **Parent-child therapy:** sessions together.
- **Family therapy:** includes siblings, parents, or even teachers.
- **Group therapy:** children with similar experiences supporting one another.

Types of Therapy

- **Behavior Therapy:** strengthens positive behaviors and reduces problem ones.
- **Cognitive-Behavioral Therapy (CBT):** helps children change negative thoughts into healthier patterns.
- **Parent Training:** equips parents with tools to support their child at home.

Do's & Don'ts for Parents

Do:

- Keep open communication with your child and their therapist.
- Encourage your child's progress and celebrate small wins.
- Stay consistent with therapy sessions and strategies.
- Respect privacy trust that the therapist will share when needed.

Don't:

- Pressure your child to "get better" quickly.
- Dismiss or minimize their feelings.
- Overstep during therapy sessions.

Parenting Tips:

- Care for yourself, too. When you are rested and supported, you can better support your child.
- Build a support system of family, friends, or groups.
- Practice patience the healing journey takes time, but every step forward matters.

Reflection Questions

- How do I present therapy as a positive resource?

- How can I support my child's progress outside of sessions?

Mental Health

Mental health is just as important as physical health. It means feeling secure, loved, and capable of handling life's challenges. Children flourish when they feel safe to express themselves and know they are supported.

Signs a Child May Be Struggling

- Declining performance at school.
- Withdrawal from activities they once enjoyed.
- Excessive worry, sadness, or irritability.
- Persistent disobedience, aggression, or tantrums.
- Loss of appetite, sleep problems, or frequent stomachaches and headaches.

Meeting Children's Emotional Needs

- Offer **unconditional love.** Remind your child that your love isn't based on achievements.
- Be honest about your own mistakes; this teaches them that everyone learns and grows.
- Celebrate effort, not just results.
- Play together regularly. Play builds bonds and helps children feel valued.
- Encourage friendships and a sense of belonging.

Creating a Safe Environment

- Maintain calm, consistent, and predictable home routines.
- Ensure children feel safe to talk openly, without fear of harsh punishment or ridicule.

- Explain the reasons behind discipline so they understand, not just obey.
- Match discipline to the behavior not too harsh, not too lenient.

Parenting Tips:

- Schedule regular play and bonding time.
- Offer encouragement daily through hugs, high-fives, or simple words like *"I believe in you."*
- Watch for signs of distress and seek professional support when needed.
- Take care of your own mental health, too. A well-supported parent can better support their child.

Reflection Questions

- What signs might show me my child is struggling emotionally?

- How do I create a safe space for them to share feelings?

Mental Health Conditions

Children, just like adults, may face challenges with their mental health. Naming and understanding these conditions helps families support their child with compassion, patience, and the proper care.

ADHD/ADD

- **ADHD (Attention Deficit Hyperactivity Disorder):** makes it harder to focus, follow directions, or sit still.
- **ADD (Attention Deficit Disorder):** more related to distractibility and forgetfulness, without as much hyperactivity.

What to Watch For:

- Trouble focusing or finishing homework.
- Forgetfulness, losing things, or seeming disorganized.
- Restlessness, fidgeting, or blurting out answers.
- Anxiety, mood swings, or low self-esteem.

How to Support:

- Seek an evaluation from a qualified professional.
- Combine strategies, including therapy, parental support, and, in some cases, medication.
- Celebrate your child's strengths and talents they are so much more than a diagnosis.
- Be patient; progress takes time and consistency.

Bipolar Disorder

A mood disorder marked by extreme highs (energy, little sleep, impulsivity) and lows (sadness, fatigue, hopelessness).

Support Steps:

- Professional evaluation and therapy.
- Medication when prescribed.
- Involve your child in decisions to help them feel respected and empowered.

Conduct Disorder

Children with conduct disorder may struggle with adhering to rules, demonstrating empathy, and respecting others' rights.

Support Steps:

- Learn about the condition.
- Seek family-centered, age-appropriate treatment.
- Partner with a mental health professional who specializes in children.

Adolescent Depression & Suicide

Depression in teens can disrupt daily life and lead to dangerous thoughts.

Warning Signs:

- Withdrawing from friends, poor school performance, loss of interest.
- Feelings of worthlessness, hopelessness, or excessive guilt.
- Discussing, writing about, or drawing about death.
- Giving away belongings.

How to Help:

- Listen more than you speak. Offer compassion, not lectures.
- Take any talk of suicide seriously ask direct questions and seek help immediately.
- Reach out to a mental health professional.
- Share resources like the **Suicide Hotline: 1-800-273-TALK (8255) or text or call 988.**

Reflection Questions

- What support systems can I put in place for my child?

- How can I help reduce stigma around mental health in my family?

Chapter 5

<u>Social Life and Community</u>

Children learn a great deal from the world around them — friendships, community, and cultural connections all shape who they become. In this section, you'll find guidance on sharing, cooperation, kindness, and celebrating differences. These lessons help children develop into compassionate, respectful individuals who value themselves and others.

Sharing

Sharing teaches children about kindness, cooperation, and friendship. It helps them understand fairness and builds the skills needed for healthy relationships.

Why Sharing Matters

- **Friendship:** Sharing builds trust and helps children form and maintain friendships.
- **Cooperation:** Learning to take turns and respect others' belongings teaches problem-solving and patience.
- **Empathy:** Sharing helps children see and care about how others feel.
- **Resilience:** It helps them cope with disappointment when things don't go their way.

Creating a Sharing Environment

- Give children chances to share at playdates, school, and group activities.
- Use games that involve turn-taking, such as board games or sports.
- Praise acts of sharing with specific encouragement: *"I love how you let your sister use your toy. That was very kind."*
- Point out when others share and highlight the positive example.

Parenting Tips:

- Explain why sharing matters: *"When you share, others are more likely to share with you too."*
- Allow children to keep a few special items private, respecting that not everything needs to be shared.
- Encourage practice in group settings if they're an only child.

Reflection Questions

- How do I encourage my child to share without forcing?

- What opportunities can I create for them to practice sharing?

Cooperation

Cooperation means working together for a common goal. It teaches children patience, teamwork, and problem-solving skills that will serve them for a lifetime.

Teaching Cooperation

- Start with small tasks, such as building a puzzle, setting the table, or cleaning a room together.
- Praise teamwork: *"You worked so well with your sister to finish that!"*
- Encourage sharing responsibility in family activities.
- Teach compromise: sometimes giving a little helps the whole group.

Benefits of Cooperation

- Builds stronger relationships.
- Reduces conflicts and arguments.
- Helps children succeed in school group projects.
- Strengthens problem-solving and leadership skills.

Parenting Tips:

- Model cooperation in your own relationships.
- Involve children in family decision-making: *"Should we cook tacos or spaghetti tonight?"*
- Remind them that cooperation doesn't mean losing it means everyone wins together.
- Celebrate successes as a team.

Reflection Questions

- What daily tasks can we practice as a team?

- How do I celebrate cooperation when I see it?

Kindness

Kindness is the language of the heart. Teaching children to be kind helps them build empathy, compassion, and a sense of belonging.

Acts of Kindness

- Saying kind words to family, friends, or teachers.
- Helping someone carry books or open a door.
- Including others in games or conversations.
- Writing thank-you notes or drawing pictures for loved ones.

Teaching Kindness

- Point out kind acts you see in daily life.
- Share stories and books that highlight kindness.
- Encourage children to notice when someone needs a smile, a hug, or a helping hand.
- Praise kindness often: *"That was so thoughtful of you."*

Parenting Tips:

- Model kindness at home—children reflect what they see.
- Remind them that kindness doesn't have to be big—it can be as small as a smile.
- Set a daily goal to practice acts of kindness as a family.
- Teach that kindness also means being kind to themselves.

Reflection Questions

- How can I encourage daily acts of kindness in my child's life?

- What kind moments can we reflect on together each day?

Listening

Listening is more than hearing words—it's paying attention with love and care. When children feel truly heard, they learn to listen with empathy as well.

Teaching Good Listening

- Model active listening by maintaining eye contact, nodding, and repeating back what you heard.
- Pause your own tasks to give your child your full attention when they speak.
- Teach turn-taking in conversations—waiting patiently while others finish speaking.
- Ask open-ended questions that invite your child to share more.

Why Listening Matters

- Builds trust between parent and child.
- Strengthens friendships and family bonds.
- Helps with problem-solving and conflict resolution.
- Shows respect for others' thoughts and feelings.

Parenting Tips:

- Put away devices during essential conversations.
- Praise listening skills: *"I love how you waited and listened carefully."*
- Encourage children to listen to both words and feelings.
- Remind them: good listeners make others feel valued.

Reflection Questions

- How can I show my child that I truly listen to them?

- What listening habits can I practice to be a better model?

Friendship

Friendship gives children a sense of belonging and joy. Good friendships teach kindness, compromise, and loyalty.

Teaching Friendship Skills

- Show children how to introduce themselves and join play respectfully.
- Encourage kindness, sharing, and fairness in their interactions.
- Teach them to apologize and forgive when conflicts happen.
- Remind them that real friends respect boundaries and lift each other up.

Supporting Healthy Friendships

- Encourage diverse friendships with children of different backgrounds and interests.
- Role-play how to handle conflict without hurting feelings.
- Teach them to walk away from friendships that are unkind or unsafe.
- Celebrate their efforts to be a good friend, not just to have friends.

Parenting Tips:

- Invite friends over to give your child chances to practice social skills.

- Model friendship in your own life let them see you support and care for others.
- Listen to their stories about friends without judgment.
- Remind them: *"It's better to have one true friend than many who don't treat you well."*

Reflection Questions

- What lessons about friendship can I share from my own life?

- How can I encourage healthy, supportive friendships for my child?

Bullying

Bullying hurts deeply, but children can learn to stand firm and feel supported with the right tools. Creating safe, loving environments at home and school is key.

Types of Bullying

- **Verbal:** teasing, name-calling, threats.
- **Physical:** hitting, pushing, taking belongings.
- **Social:** excluding others, spreading rumors.
- **Cyberbullying:** hurtful messages or posts online.

Helping a Child Who's Being Bullied

- Listen calmly and thank them for sharing their thoughts.
- Reassure them it's not their fault.
- Role-play responses: walking away, using strong body language, or seeking help.
- Involve teachers, counselors, or administrators when needed.

Preventing Bullying

- Teach respect and kindness at home.
- Encourage empathy: *"How would you feel if that happened to you?"*
- Praise acts of inclusion and standing up for others.
- Monitor social media and online activity thoughtfully, with open and respectful conversations.

Parenting Tips:

- Let your child know they are never alone—you are always in their corner.
- Celebrate their courage in speaking up.
- Remind them that asking for help shows strength, not weakness.
- Encourage friendships with peers who uplift and support them.

Reflection Questions

- How do I respond calmly if my child tells me they're being bullied?

- What tools can I give them to stand strong and seek help?

Social Skills

Strong social skills help children build healthy friendships, work well with others, and feel confident in new situations.

Teaching Social Skills

- Practice greetings, introductions, and polite conversation.
- Encourage sharing, turn-taking, and cooperation.
- Teach active listening: maintain eye contact, nod, and respond in a kind and considerate manner.
- Role-play scenarios like joining a group at recess or asking to play.

Building Friendships

- Invite friends over for playdates or activities.
- Encourage involvement in clubs, sports, or community programs.
- Help them navigate conflicts with kindness and honesty.

Parenting Tips:

- Model positive interactions in your own relationships.
- Praise respectful and friendly behavior when you see it.
- Guide them gently when mistakes occur, rather than criticizing.
- Remind them that friendships take effort, patience, and care.

Reflection Questions

- How do I help my child practice kindness and cooperation?

- What new opportunities can I give them to build friendships?

Manners

Manners are everyday kindnesses that make others feel respected and valued. Teaching them helps children shine in social situations and build lasting relationships.

Everyday Manners

- Saying "please" and "thank you."
- Greeting others with a smile or a kind word.
- Waiting for their turn to speak.
- Respecting personal space.

Table Manners

- Chewing with their mouths closed.
- Saying *"May I be excused?"* before leaving the table.
- Helping set and clear the table.

Parenting Tips:

- Model manners daily children learn best by watching you.
- Gently remind instead of scolding. *"Try asking with 'please.'"*
- Praise polite behavior: *"That was very respectful of you."*
- Explain the "why," manners aren't just rules; they make people feel cared for.

Reflection Questions

- How do I model good manners for my child?

- What polite habits should we focus on as a family?

Helping Others

Helping others teaches children empathy, responsibility, and the joy of giving. It reminds them that even small acts of kindness can make a big difference.

Ways Kids Can Help

- Do small chores for family or neighbors.
- Volunteer in age-appropriate ways, like food drives or park clean-ups.
- Offer friendship and support to classmates who are left out.
- Share skills or talents reading to younger children, drawing cards, or baking treats.
-

Parenting Tips:

- Encourage helping without expecting something in return.
- Praise the effort, not just the outcome.
- Make helping a family tradition like serving at a shelter together.
- Remind them that helping others also makes us feel good inside.

Reflection Questions

- What opportunities do I give my child to serve others?

- How can we make helping part of our family's identity?

<u>Family</u>

Family is a child's first community, where love, respect, and a sense of belonging are learned. Strong family bonds give children security and shape their values.

Strengthening Family Bonds

- Share meals together whenever possible.
- Create family traditions for holidays, birthdays, or simple Friday nights.
- Encourage open conversations where everyone's voice matters.
- Celebrate milestones big and small together.

The Role of Family

- Provides unconditional love and support.
- Teaches life lessons and cultural traditions.
- Offers a safe place to practice kindness, responsibility, and forgiveness.
- Gives children their first examples of healthy relationships.

Parenting Tips:

- Spend intentional time together quality matters more than quantity.

- Resolve conflicts respectfully so that children learn healthy problem-solving skills.

- Show affection: openly hugs, kind words, and encouragement strengthen bonds.

- Remind children often: *"No matter what happens, you always belong here."*

Reflection Questions

- What traditions bring my family closer together?

- How can I show my child that they always belong here?

Religion / Beliefs

Faith and beliefs give children a sense of purpose, hope, and belonging. Whether through religion, spirituality, or family values, guiding children in this area helps them grow with integrity and compassion.

Teaching Faith and Values

- Share your family's beliefs in age-appropriate ways.
- Include children in traditions like prayers, rituals, or celebrations.
- Encourage questions curiosity is part of learning.
- Show respect for other people's beliefs and differences.

Why It Matters

- Provides comfort and guidance in difficult times.
- Builds community and connection.
- Helps children develop morals, compassion, and gratitude.
- Encourages a more profound sense of identity and purpose.

Parenting Tips:

- Model your beliefs in daily actions kindness, honesty, service, and love.
- Involve children in giving or service projects that reflect your values.
- Respect their growing independence allow them space to explore and reflect on their own.
- Remind them that beliefs can be both deeply personal and shared with others.

Reflection Questions

- What beliefs or values do I want to pass on?

- How do I model respect for others' beliefs?

Cultural Differences

Every family, every child, and every community carries a beautiful story. From the shade of our skin to the sounds of our language, from our faith to our food, we are surrounded by rich differences that make the world vibrant and full of life.

Even babies as young as six months begin to notice differences in faces and voices. As they grow, children naturally become curious about the world around them, race, culture, religion, ability, and family structure. That curiosity isn't something to hush; it's something to celebrate and guide with love.

When caregivers openly talk about diversity, they help children develop empathy, respect, and appreciation for others and pride in who they are.

Why Cultural Awareness Matters

- Builds empathy and understanding for people who are different.
- Encourages pride in one's own culture and curiosity about others.
- Reduces prejudice and bullying by fostering respect.
- Prepares children to thrive in diverse schools, workplaces, and communities.

Share Your Family Culture

Help your child understand where they come from by sharing your own story. Talk about your family's traditions, heritage, and the values that shaped you.

- Share family recipes, dances, and songs.
- Teach them about meaningful holidays, heroes, and historical figures.
- Tell stories about your ancestors and where they came from.

When children see that their own background is valued, they are more likely to value others too.

Expose Them to Different Music and Art

Music and art open hearts in ways words cannot.

- Introduce instruments, songs, and rhythms from around the world.
- Listen to music in different languages or styles.
- Visit art festivals or cultural museums.

Encouraging exploration teaches your child that beauty comes in many forms, just like people.

Encourage Questions

When your child asks about differences, it's a moment for learning, not silence.

- Let them know it's okay to notice and talk about what they see.
- Give honest, simple explanations that focus on kindness and respect.
- For example, if your child asks, "Why is she in a wheelchair?" you can say, "She uses the wheelchair to help her move because her legs work differently. Everyone's

body is unique, and that's what makes people special."

- Questions open doors to understanding, don't close them.

Address Stereotypes and Biases

Children begin forming ideas about people long before they truly understand them. Help them build fairness and compassion by:

- Reading age-appropriate books that show diverse families and heroes.
- Watching inclusive media together and talking about what you see.
- Discussing stereotypes gently and helping your child think critically.
- Encourage your child to focus on what people *can do*, not what they can't.

Celebrate Their Culture

Cultural pride builds confidence and belonging.

- Plan multicultural family nights where you explore new foods or traditions.
- Attend community festivals or heritage celebrations.
- Display family photos, symbols, or flags proudly in your home.
- When children know their roots, they stand taller and they'll respect the roots of others too.

Encourage Inclusive Friendships

Guide your child to build friendships across different races, religions, abilities, and backgrounds.

- Diversity in friendships helps children see that kindness and connection go beyond appearances.
- Encourage them to include others and to stand up for peers who may be treated unfairly.
- The world grows gentler every time a child makes a friend who is different from them.

Be the Example

Children learn inclusion best by watching the adults around them.

- Speak up against bias and unkindness.
- Show respect to people from all walks of life.
- Focus on the strengths and stories that make each person unique.
- You are your child's first and most powerful role model. Your words and actions shape how they see others.

Great Children's Books on Diversity and Identity:

  i. **Diversity**: "It's Okay to be Different"
 ii. **Acceptance**: "The Skin You Live in"
iii. **Culture Geography**: "Same, Same but Different"
 iv. **Religion**: "Where Does God Live?"
  v. **Disabilities**: "Don't Call Me Special"
 vi. **Different Family Configurations**: "The Family Book"

Parenting Tips:

- Share your own family traditions with pride.
- Expose children to books, music, and foods from different cultures.
- Encourage friendships with children from diverse backgrounds.
- Visit cultural festivals, museums, or community events together.
- Remind them: *"Different doesn't mean wrong, it means we can learn something new."*

Reflection Questions

- How do I honor and share my family's cultural background with my child?

- What opportunities can I create for my child to learn about other cultures?

Chapter 6

<u>Responsibility and Life Skills</u>

Children flourish when they are trusted with responsibility and given the tools to care for themselves and their world. In this section, you'll explore skills like chores, hygiene, budgeting, and managing money. These practical lessons build independence, confidence, and a strong sense of contribution.

Responsibility

Responsibility is about doing what needs to be done and taking ownership of choices. Teaching children responsibility builds independence, self-respect, and trust.

Building Responsibility

- Give age-appropriate chores or tasks.
- Encourage them to manage schoolwork with gentle support.
- Teach natural consequences when something is forgotten, they help fix it.
- Show them that responsibility includes caring for themselves, others, and their environment.

Signs of Growing Responsibility

- Following through without reminders.
- Admitting mistakes and working to correct them.
- Showing pride in a job well done.
- Caring for personal belongings.

Parenting Tips:

- Praise responsibility with specific words: *"You remembered to feed the dog without me asking, that's responsible."*
- Be patient, responsibility grows over time with practice.
- Model responsibility in your own life: paying bills on time, keeping promises, caring for your home.
- Allow mistakes as learning opportunities, not failures.

Reflection Questions

- What responsibilities help my child feel trusted?

- How do I respond when they make mistakes?

Chores

Chores aren't just about keeping the house clean; they help children learn responsibility, teamwork, and independence.

Why Chores Matter

- Teach responsibility and accountability.
- Show children that they are important contributors to the family.
- Build life skills they will need as adults.

Age-Appropriate Chores

- **Ages 3–5:** put toys away, water plants, help feed pets.
- **Ages 6–9:** set the table, fold towels, sweep floors.
- **Ages 10–12:** wash dishes, vacuum, help cook simple meals.
- **Teens:** laundry, yard work, grocery shopping.

Parenting Tips:

- Work alongside your child at first to teach the task.
- Use checklists or charts to maintain consistent routines.
- Praise their effort and celebrate progress.
- Remind them that chores are a team effort: *"When we all help, the house feels happy and calm."*

Reflection Questions

- How do I make chores feel like teamwork instead of punishment?

- What new tasks is my child ready to take on?

How to Clean

Learning to clean isn't just about chores—it's about responsibility, teamwork, and pride in caring for your space. When children view cleaning as a life skill, rather than a punishment, they develop confidence and independence.

Teaching Cleaning Step by Step

- Start young with simple tasks, such as putting toys in a basket, wiping a table, or making the bed.
- Break bigger chores into smaller steps so they don't feel overwhelming.
- Clean together at first, modeling makes it easier for them to learn.

Making Cleaning Fun

- Turn on music and clean as a family "dance party."
- Set timers and race to beat the clock.
- Use colorful supplies to make the task feel special.

Parenting Tips:

- Praise effort, not perfection. *"I love how you tried folding the towels yourself!"*
- Assign age-appropriate chores and gradually increase responsibility.
- Teach natural consequences: *"When we don't wash dishes, they pile up and get smelly."*
- Show them that cleaning is an act of self-respect and care for the whole family.

Reflection Questions

- How can I make cleaning a fun, shared activity?

- What chores can I introduce that build confidence?

Hygiene

Good hygiene is more than staying clean; it's about self-respect, health, and confidence. Teaching children healthy routines early helps them feel comfortable in their growing bodies.

Encouraging Healthy Habits

- Start early: let toddlers practice brushing teeth or washing hands with your guidance.
- Encourage independence as they grow by ages 6–9; most children can manage their daily routines independently.
- Model good hygiene yourself; children copy what they see.

Conversations About Hygiene

- Keep discussions ongoing. As your child grows, introduce new habits (like flossing or skincare).
- Normalize puberty and body changes as natural parts of growing up.
- Be gentle with sensitive topics. Approach them with love and reassurance.

Parenting Tips:

- Use charts or stickers to make routines more fun for younger children.
- Offer small incentives when necessary, but emphasize that hygiene is about self-care, not a reward system.
- Avoid nagging or shaming. Gentle reminders build confidence, not embarrassment.

- Teach practical consequences: *"When we don't brush teeth, cavities can form."*
- Respect cultural and personal differences in hair and body care.

Reflection Questions

- How can I make hygiene routines positive and encouraging?

- What new habits is my child ready to learn?

Budgeting

Budgeting is about making wise choices with money so it serves you rather than controls you. Teaching children money skills early prepares them for independence and confidence.

Teaching Kids About Money

- Give small allowances and encourage saving, spending, and giving.
- Show them how to divide money into jars or envelopes labeled Save, Spend, and Share.
- Let older children help plan a grocery trip within a budget.
- Talk about needs versus wants in everyday life.

Why Budgeting Matters

- Builds responsibility and independence.
- Helps children avoid debt and overspending later in life.
- Teaches patience and planning for future goals.
- Encourages generosity when they budget for giving.

Parenting Tips:

- Model healthy money habits: pay bills on time, save regularly, and give generously.
- Celebrate when your child reaches a savings goal.
- Be honest about financial limits without fear or shame.
- Remind them: *"Money is a tool, not the goal; it's how we use it that matters."*

Reflection Questions

- How can I introduce money management in everyday life?

- What habits can I model about saving and spending?

Finances

Understanding money helps children make wise choices and feel secure about their future. Teaching financial skills early sets them up for independence and confidence.

Building Financial Awareness

- Talk openly about money, don't make it a secret.
- Demonstrate how banks, checks, debit cards, and credit card's function.
- Involving older children in family budgeting discussions can be beneficial.
- Teach the importance of saving before spending.

Why It Matters

- Prevents money stress later in life.
- Builds responsibility and planning skills.
- Helps children distinguish between needs and wants.
- Encourages generosity and wise giving.

Parenting Tips:

- Share your own financial habits and lessons learned.
- Use real-life examples, like comparing prices at the store.
- Encourage goal setting, saving for a toy, trip, or gift.
- Remind them: *"Money is a tool to support your life, not the measure of your worth."*

Reflection Questions

- How can I prepare my child to be financially responsible?

- What money lessons do I want them to learn from me?

Taxes

Taxes may seem like a grown-up topic, but children benefit from learning early why they matter. Explaining taxes in simple, favorable terms helps kids understand the importance of responsibility and community.

Making Taxes Real for Kids

- Show them your paycheck and explain why money is taken out.
- Point out taxes on shopping receipts.
- Visit parks, libraries, or schools and explain: *"These places are here because of taxes."*
- Volunteer at community services so children can see tax dollars at work.

Parenting Tips:

- Speak positively about taxes: they help build safe, healthy communities.
- File taxes on time and model responsibility.
- Explain different kinds of taxes sales tax, income tax, property tax in kid-friendly language.
- Have honest conversations about money, saving, and planning for the future.

Reflection Questions

- How can I explain taxes in a way that feels meaningful to my child?

- What real-life examples of community benefits can I show them?

Nutrition and Physical Health

Healthy eating and active living give children the energy, strength, and focus they need to thrive. When we model good habits, they learn to care for their own bodies with love and respect.

Why Nutrition Matters

Food fuels the body and mind. Balanced nutrition helps kids grow strong, fight illness, and feel energized.

The **five food groups** are:

- **Fruits:** Rich in vitamins that protect against illness.
- **Vegetables:** Packed with minerals and fiber for strength and healing.
- **Grains:** Provide energy and help digestion.
- **Protein:** Builds muscles and keeps the body strong.
- **Dairy:** Strengthens bones and provides essential vitamins.

Fun Ideas for Meals & Snacks

- **Fruits:** smoothies, parfaits, or colorful fruit salads.
- **Veggies**: crunchy raw veggies with dip, soups, or pasta dishes.
- **Grains:** oatmeal, rice bowls, or baked potatoes.
- **Protein:** grilled chicken, eggs, or fish.
- **Dairy:** yogurt parfaits or milk in smoothies.

Physical Activity

Children's bodies and minds grow stronger with movement.

Activity builds confidence, improves focus in school, and boosts happiness.

- Kids need about **one hour of active play or exercise each day.**
- Young children benefit from free play, such as running, jumping, and climbing.
- Older kids can enjoy sports, biking, swimming, or strength activities.

Parenting Tips:

- Be the example, let your kids see you making healthy food choices and staying active.
- Make meals colorful, "eat the rainbow."
- Don't force foods. Encourage exploration and patience with picky eaters.
- Keep activity fun: family walks, bike rides, or dance parties in the living room.
- Remind kids that balance matters; it's okay to enjoy treats in moderation.

Reflection Questions

- How can I make healthy habits fun for my child?

- What healthy habits do I already model well?

Chapter 7

<u>Preparing for the Future</u>

As children grow, they begin looking ahead to bigger responsibilities and dreams. This section examines health, work, education, and the challenges of adolescence, including the impact of social media and peer pressure. With your love and guidance, children can step into the future with confidence and a sense of purpose.

Work Ethic

A strong work ethic means taking pride in doing your best, even when a task is challenging and demanding. Teaching this skill helps children succeed in school, in their relationships, and in life.

Building Work Ethic

- Encourage them to finish what they start, even if it's tough.
- Praise effort, not just results. *"I'm proud of how hard you worked on that project."*
- Teach responsibility through daily chores and schoolwork.
- Share stories of people who achieved goals through persistence.

Parenting Tips:

- Model hard work, let your children see you doing your best at your own tasks.
- Avoid rescuing them from every struggle; challenges build resilience.
- Celebrate small wins but remind them that success often takes time and consistency.
- Encourage teamwork: *"When we all work together, things get done faster."*

Reflection Questions

- What responsibilities can help my child build pride their efforts?

- How can I praise persistence instead of only results?

Work / Jobs

Teaching children the value of work helps them develop a sense of responsibility, pride, and independence. Work isn't just about money; it's about contribution and growth.

Introducing Work to Kids

- Start with small household jobs: feeding pets, watering plants, or taking out the trash.
- As they grow, give them bigger responsibilities, such as babysitting, mowing lawns, or part-time jobs.
- Encourage them to explore careers through volunteering, internships, or shadowing.

Lessons Learned Through Work

- Responsibility and accountability.
- Time management and organization.
- Teamwork and communication.
- The satisfaction of earning and contributing.

Parenting Tips:

- Celebrate their efforts in every job, no matter how small.
- Teach balance work is essential, but so are rest and play.
- Share stories of your first jobs and what you learned.
- Remind them: *"Every job teaches you something valuable."*

Reflection Questions

- What first jobs or tasks can teach my child responsibility?

- How do I model a healthy balance between work and rest?

<u>Success</u>

Success means more than achievements; it's about doing your best, growing through challenges, and finding joy in the journey.

Teaching True Success

- Celebrate effort, persistence, and learning, not just results.
- Encourage children to set realistic goals.
- Remind them that success looks different for everyone.
- Teach them to view mistakes as stepping stones, not failures.

Why It Matters

- Builds resilience and confidence.
- Helps children develop a growth mindset.
- Encourages them to define success by values, not comparisons.
- Inspires pride in hard work and perseverance.

Parenting Tips:

- Share your own successes and failures as learning examples.
- Praise character traits, kindness, honesty, and courage alongside achievements.
- Help them reflect: *"What did you learn from this experience?"*
- Remind them: *"Success isn't about being perfect, it's about growing."*

Reflection Questions

- How can I teach my child that success is more than achievements?

- What story from my life can I share about persistence and growth?

Purpose

Purpose gives children direction and meaning. It helps them recognize their unique gifts and how to use them to make the world a better place.

Helping Children Discover Purpose

- Encourage exploration through sports, arts, science, and volunteering.
- Celebrate their talents and passions, even if they're different from your own.
- Teach them that mistakes and setbacks are stepping stones, not roadblocks.
- Connect purpose to service: *"Your gift can bring joy to others."*

Why Purpose Matters

- Builds resilience during challenges.
- Strengthens confidence and motivation.
- Helps children feel they belong and have value.
- Creates a foundation for future goals and dreams.

Parenting Tips:

- Share stories of people who found purpose through perseverance.
- Remind your child their purpose doesn't have to be big, it can be as simple as being kind or helpful each day.
- Encourage journaling, art, or prayer to explore a more profound meaning.
- Celebrate progress, not perfection, on their journey.

Reflection Questions

- How can I encourage my child to discover their gifts?

- What examples can I share of finding meaning in life?

Education

Education is more than learning facts and figures; it's about helping children develop curiosity, confidence, and a lifelong love of learning. Early experiences in school and at home shape how children view themselves as learners, and the support they receive from caregivers makes all the difference.

The Importance of Early Childhood Education

Early childhood is a time of rapid growth. In these years, children begin to develop skills that form the foundation for future success — not just in school, but in life as well. Through play, interaction, and guided learning, children grow physically, emotionally, socially, and cognitively.

- They begin to explore numbers, letters, colors, and stories.
- They practice independence through self-help skills.
- They learn to recognize and manage their emotions in healthy ways.
- They meet children from diverse backgrounds, fostering understanding and respect among them.
- They practice cooperation, teamwork, and kindness.
- When children are given the opportunity to learn and explore early, they develop confidence in their abilities and become comfortable in a community of peers.

The Benefits of Education

A strong education provides more than academics. It helps children:

- Grow in independence and responsibility.

- Develop teamwork and cooperation skills.

- Respect cultural differences and celebrate their own traditions.

- Strengthen communication and social skills.

- Expand their knowledge of the world around them.

- See themselves as valuable members of their community.

- Gain confidence to pursue their goals and dreams.

Supporting a Love of Learning at Home

Learning doesn't stop at the classroom door; it begins at home. Caregivers can nurture a child's love of learning by creating a safe, supportive environment where questions are welcomed and mistakes are seen as part of the learning journey.

Parenting Tips:

- **Unlink fear and learning.** Avoid using threats or shame about education. Instead, bring humor, encouragement, and structure to the learning process. Show that learning can be fun.

- **Celebrate curiosity.** Remind your child that there are no "silly" questions. Questions are how we learn.

- **Praise effort, not just results.** Recognize the hard work your child puts into learning, even if they make mistakes. Reassurance builds resilience.

- **Make learning part of daily life.** Talk about what you're reading, cooking, or observing outside. Ask, *"What did you learn today?"*

- **Read together.** Reading aloud helps spark imagination and builds language skills.

- **Normalize failure.** Let your child know that mistakes are a natural part of the learning process. Share your own stories of learning through failure.

- **Use music.** Many children concentrate better with gentle background music. Try playing instrumental music during study times.

Helping Your Child Succeed in School

There are many ways caregivers can partner with schools to support a child's education:

- Attend back-to-school nights and parent–teacher conferences to stay connected and informed.

- Visit the school or its website to become familiar with staff, resources, and events.

- Support healthy homework habits with a distraction-free study space.

- Send your child to school ready to learn — with a good breakfast, enough rest, and a sense of routine.

- Teach organizational skills, such as keeping folders, planners, and desks tidy.

- Introduce study skills early: break large tasks into smaller ones, study ahead of time, and use memory aids.

- Familiarize yourself with your child's school rules and disciplinary policies and collaborate with teachers as a team.

- Get involved by volunteering or attending school events.

- Take attendance seriously consistent presence builds consistency in learning.

- Discuss school experiences daily, showing genuine interest and care.

- These everyday actions send a powerful message: *education matters, and you are not alone in it.*

Reflection Questions

- How do I encourage curiosity and a love of learning in my child?

- What routines can I create at home to support focus, rest, and study?

- How do I show my child that mistakes are part of the learning process?

- In what ways can I become more connected with my child's school and teachers?

College

College can be an exciting path for growth, learning, and opportunity, but it's just one of many options for building a meaningful future. Helping children explore their choices with confidence sets them up for success.

Preparing for College

- Encourage curiosity and a love of learning from an early age.
- Talk about different paths: community college, trade schools, apprenticeships, and universities.
- Visit campuses, attend career fairs, or explore virtual tours together.
- Teach them how to balance academics with self-care and social life.

Supporting Their Journey

- Remind them college is about more than grades—it's about discovering passions, friendships, and purpose.
- Celebrate progress, not just acceptance letters.
- Offer guidance with applications, scholarships, and financial aid.
- Respect their independence as they make choices for their future.

Parenting Tips:

- Share your own experiences, including the challenges you've faced and the lessons you've learned.
- Encourage responsibility in managing time, money, and commitments.
- Remind them: *"Whatever path you choose, I believe in you."*

Reflection Questions

- How can I support my child's choices about education or career?

- What encouragement can I offer if their path looks different from mine?

Handling Peer Pressure

Peer pressure is a normal part of growing up, but it can feel overwhelming for children. Teaching kids to trust themselves and make their own choices helps them stand firm in challenging situations.

Helping Kids Handle Peer Pressure

- Remind them it's okay to say *"no"* when something feels wrong.
- Role-play scenarios to practice responding.
- Encourage them to consider the consequences before making decisions.
- Build their confidence so they don't feel they must follow the crowd.

Positive Peer Pressure

- Point out that peer pressure can be good, too, like encouraging each other to study, try out for a sport, or be kind.
- Celebrate when your child chooses friends who inspire them to do better.

Parenting Tips:

- Maintain open communication, ask about their friends and what's happening at school.
- Support their individuality so they feel less dependent on others' approval.

- Teach phrases like, *"No thanks, that's not for me,"* or *"I'd rather do something else."*
- Remind them: true friends respect boundaries.

Reflection Questions

- How can I prepare my child to say no with confidence?

- What positive peer influences can I encourage?

Social Media

Social media can connect and inspire, but it can also bring challenges like anxiety, poor sleep, or unhealthy comparisons. Guiding children with honesty and boundaries helps them use technology wisely.

Helping Kids Navigate Social Media

- Delay access as long as possible and introduce apps only when they show maturity.
- Create a family plan to discuss privacy, safety, and respectful online behavior.
- Encourage open conversations about what they're seeing and experiencing.
- Keep devices out of bedrooms to protect sleep.

Parenting Tips:

- Set time limits: The American Academy of Pediatrics recommends limiting screen use for young children to about 1 hour daily for ages 3–4.
- Talk openly about unrealistic beauty standards, peer pressure, and online comparisons.
- Monitor your own screen time; children learn balance by watching you.
- Remind them: *"Likes or followers don't measure your worth, you are valuable just as you are."*

Reflection Questions

- How can I guide my child toward healthy social media habits?

- What conversations can I have about online safety and self-worth?

Drugs & Alcohol

As children grow into adolescence, they may face pressures around drugs and alcohol. These conversations can feel uncomfortable, but starting them early helps build trust and enables children to make safe, confident choices.

Teaching Awareness and Responsibility

- Begin talking about drugs and alcohol before your child faces peer pressure.
- Use age-appropriate language and focus on safety, health, and respect for the body.
- Explain how substances affect the brain and body in simple, clear terms.
- Emphasize that mistakes can happen, but honesty and asking for help are always welcome.

Parenting Tips:

- Keep communication open and judgment-free your child should feel safe asking questions.
- Set clear family expectations while explaining the reasons behind them.
- Model healthy choices about alcohol, medication, and stress management.
- Practice refusal skills together by role-playing saying "no" in real-life scenarios.
- Reassure them: *"You never have to face peer pressure alone, I'm always here for you."*

Reflection Questions

- How can I create a safe space for my child to ask questions about drugs and alcohol?

- What healthy coping skills can I teach to help them handle stress without substances?

Closing Message

Caring for children is one of the most meaningful journeys you will ever take. It is filled with joys, challenges, laughter, and lessons that shape both you and the children you love. This handbook is not meant to provide you with all the answers, but to remind you that you already possess what matters most: love, patience, and the willingness to keep learning. No matter your role, parent, grandparent, guardian, or foster parent, your care makes an immeasurable difference. Remember, you don't have to do it all perfectly. You have to do it with love.

Resources

1. **Anglin, J. (2024)**. How to Teach Your Kids About Taxes. February 2, 2024.

2. **Centers for Disease Control and Prevention (CDC)**. STDs & STIs. Retrieved from https://www.cdc.gov/std/default.htm

3. **How to Teach Children About Cultural Awareness and Diversity**. PBS Kids Parenting.

4. **Kostecki-Shaw, J. S**. Same, Same but Different.

5. **Parr, T.** Don't Call Me Special.

6. **Parr, T.** It's Okay to Be Different.

7. **Parr, T.** The Family Book.

8. **Tyler, M.** The Skin You Live In.

9. **Where Does God Live?** Holly Bea.

10. **The use of social media in Children and Adolescents: Scoping Review on the Potential Risks.** PubMed Central (PMC), August 12, 2022.

11. **How Social Media Affects Your Teen's Mental Health: A Parent's Guide.** Yale Medicine.

12. **Popular YouTube Educational Videos** — e.g., Ms. Rachel.

13. **World Health Organization (WHO)**. Sexual Health.

Retrieved from https://www.who.int/health-topics/sexual-health.

14. **How to teach moral values to kids?** Orchidadmin, September 5, 2023, Orchid's The International School.

Citations

1. Anglin, J. (2024, February 2). "How to teach your kids about taxes."

2. Bobo, A. (2022, January 25). "3 tips for respecting your child's boundaries."

3. Blumberg Capman, P. O., & Thomas, J. (2023, June 28). "The five apology languages: The secret to healthy relationships."

4. Boys and Girls Club of America. (2022, June 17). "Ways to build trust between parents and teens".

5. Cullins, A. (2022, October). "Key strategies to teach children empathy (sorted by age)." Big Life Journal.

6. Cruze, R. "15 ways to teach kids about money." GoHenry.com.

7. "Connecticut Alliance to End Sexual Violence." (2024). "8 ways to teach kids about consent and healthy boundaries."

8. Hallowell, E. M. (n.d.). "Practical tips to help your child learn better and value education."

9. Hirsch, L. (n.d.). "10 ways to help your child succeed in elementary school."

10. Johnson, K. (2023, January 31). "How to talk to your child about sex and reproductive health."

11. Mitchell, K. (n.d.). "Age-appropriate sex talks: When to have these conversations."

12. McCutchen, D. (2023, February 14). "How to teach your kids

about healthy relationships."

13. Merk, L. (2023, December 12). "8 ways parents can teach kindness to kids."

14. Mental Health of America, Inc. (MHA). (2024).

15. Orchidadmin. (2023, September 5). "How to teach moral values to kids?"

16. Orchinik, L. J. (n.d.). "Teaching kids not to bully."

17. Patel, M. (n.d.). "The importance of kids' education: Building the future."

18. PMC (PubMed Central). (2022, August 12). "The use of social media in children and adolescents: Scoping review on the potential risks."

19. "PBS Kids Parenting." "How to teach children about cultural awareness and diversity."

20. Slaltengren, K. (n.d.). "Teaching kids who they can trust." Priceless Parenting.

21. "Stressful experiences: How to help your child heal." (2023). American Academy of Pediatrics.

22. "Healthychildren.org." (2021). "Childhood trauma: 3 ways to help kids cope." American Academy of Pediatrics and Pediatric Approach to trauma, treatment, and resilience.

23. Leatherwood Cannon, S. (2021, April 20). "6 tips for teaching your child about personal hygiene." Henry Ford.

24. "Vivvi, TM." (2021, September 27). "5 strategies for teaching kids about patience."

25. University of Rochester Medical Center. (n.d.). "Talking with your kids about drugs, alcohol, and tobacco."

26. Yale Medicine. "How social media affects your teen's mental health: A parent's guide."

About the Author

Vanessa Dargan is passionate about helping children and families thrive. A graduate of the University of Southern California with a degree in Human Performance and a minor in Entrepreneurship, she was captain of the USC Track and Field team and the 2015 Pac-12 Champion in the 400m. Vanessa also competed in the 2016 Olympic Trials, an experience that shaped her understanding of discipline, resilience, and perseverance.

After her collegiate and athletic career, Vanessa began coaching track and working as a personal trainer in 2017. She went on to serve as a Youth Development Professional at the Boys and Girls Club, where her love for mentoring young people deepened. In 2021, she earned her certification in Physical Education and spent two years teaching middle and high school students. Today, she serves as Assistant Director of Extended Learning and Summer Programs, continuing her mission to guide, support, and inspire youth.

Beyond her professional life, Vanessa is a family-oriented individual who values spending time with her husband, Reginald, and their loved ones. She enjoys dancing, traveling, and brunching with friends. Through every role she holds, teacher, coach, leader, and author, Vanessa's heart remains rooted in encouraging children and caregivers to grow with love, resilience, and joy.